CW00960797

*Help for the
High Street Witch*

Help for the High Street Witch

John Boon

Illustrated by Lynne Byrnes

HODDER AND STOUGHTON
LONDON   SYDNEY   AUCKLAND   TORONTO

British Library Cataloguing in Publication Data

Boon, John
  Help for the High Street witch.—(Brock
  red)
  I. Title   II. Byrnes, Lynne   III. Series
  823'.914[J]   PZ7

  ISBN 0-340-38559-6

Published by Hodder and Stoughton Children's Books,
a division of Hodder and Stoughton Ltd,
Mill Road, Dunton Green, Sevenoaks, Kent TN13 2YJ

Photoset by Rowland Phototypesetting Ltd,
Bury St Edmunds, Suffolk

Printed in Great Britain by T. J. Press (Padstow) Ltd,
Padstow, Cornwall

Contents

1   *Supersonic Moggy*

Bronwen Smith unlocked the door of her shop from the inside, turned over the card on the door so that it read 'Open', then stood for a few moments gazing out at the busy High Street, as people hurried by on their way to work. A few of them stopped to look through the small panes of glass in the old-fashioned window at the display of micro-wave cauldrons, high-performance plastic broomsticks and SpelComputers, all sprayed with artificial cobwebs and deco-rated with plastic cats, bats and spiders.

The young witch had already been hard at work since soon after six o'clock, making up potions specially ordered by customers and to replenish her stocks of everyday potions like Hair Restorer, Wart Remover and Anti-Gravity Butter Additive, to stop toast falling on the carpet butter side down.

Bronwen sighed wearily and returned to

the workroom at the rear of the shop. She looked at her list, and had just finished typing 'CURE: ACNE' on her SpelComputer's keyboard when the phone rang. She sighed again and watched the recipe appear on the computer's screen as she picked up the phone.

'Witches' Cauldron, can I help you?' she said.

'You've *got* to help me!' cried a panic-stricken voice. 'Oh, it's dreadful! That poor animal! He'll be killed!'

'Who is this?' asked Bronwen.

'It's Mrs Mortimer. I bought a "Home Witch" outfit from you, and something's gone wrong with a spell and I don't know what to do!'

'All right, Mrs Mortimer,' said Bronwen. 'Don't worry. Give me your address and I'll be there in a few minutes.'

A man was just coming into the shop when she hurried through to lock the door. 'Sorry, sir,' she said, gently but firmly pushing him back outside again. 'Emergency. Come back later.'

Back in the workroom she grabbed her emergency bag and called to her personal broomstick, who was dozing in a corner. He ignored her. She knew perfectly well that he had heard her, because his snoring had become deliberately louder.

But Bronwen was not in the mood to argue. She was tired, she had just lost a customer, and she would undoubtedly lose several more before she returned to the shop. She picked up the broomstick, opened the back door, and threw him out into the back yard as hard as she could.

His eyes flicked open and widened in alarm an instant before he hurtled into the dustbins with a tremendous clatter and a shriek of fright. There was more clattering as he extricated himself, and his handle emerged from amongst the bins.

'What did you do that for?' he howled indignantly.

'Because it's where you belong!' snapped Bronwen. 'You're lazy, good-for-nothing rubbish! I warned you the other day I'd turn you into a dustbin if you didn't behave yourself, didn't I?'

'I was asleep!' protested the broomstick. 'How am I supposed to know we've got to go and unmix Mrs Mortimer's spell if you don't wake me up and tell me?'

'Come here,' ordered Bronwen, her voice ominously quiet.

'What are you going to . . .?' quavered the broomstick.

'COME HERE!' roared Bronwen, pointing to a spot in mid-air, just in front of her. She did not really want to destroy an expensive broomstick who performed excellently when he was not being awkward, but she simply must put a stop to his bad behaviour somehow.

The broomstick knocked over two more dustbins in his hurry to obey her, and stood quivering with fright in front of her.

'Please don't melt me down! I'll be good! I'll do whatever . . .!'

He gulped and backed off hurriedly as Bronwen thrust her angry face forward. '*I* never said anything about Mrs Mortimer getting a spell wrong!' she hissed. '*You've* got pretty sharp ears for someone who was supposed to be asleep!'

She grabbed the broomstick and leapt astride it. 'Get going!'

The broomstick had never moved so fast, and they were in the air for less than a minute before Bronwen angled him steeply down. She could see Mrs Mortimer standing on her lawn. There were people in most of the nearby gardens, and still more at upstairs windows. They were all looking up, their heads moving from side to side, as if they were watching a gigantic aerial tennis match.

Nobody noticed Bronwen.

Then, as they swooped down over the roof of the house, Bronwen instinctively ducked as something streaked past her head. The next moment she found herself sprawling at Mrs Mortimer's feet. Mrs Mortimer leapt back in fright, then peered down at Bronwen.

'Oh, it's you, Miss Smith!' She helped Bronwen up and brushed some lawn clippings from her. 'Did you come by telepathy or something?'

'No,' smiled Bronwen. 'I don't usually arrive like that, but we nearly hit something as we came down, and I think it made my broomstick misjudge his landing.'

But when she pointed to the broomstick, who was standing nearby, there was more than a suspicion of a smirk on his face, so perhaps it was not exactly an accident after all.

'What on earth was that?' she exclaimed, as something flashed overhead with a sharp crack, a dull rumble, a sprinkling of water and a strange receding yowl.

'It's my poor little Doey!' wailed a voice behind her.

Bronwen turned, to find a tearful, angry-looking woman glaring at her over the garden fence.

'Doey?'

'Do-Little, her cat,' whispered Mrs Mortimer 'He may be Do-Little when he's in her garden, but he's always scratching holes in *my* flowerbeds. I thought I'd use one of the spells in my "Home Witch Outfit" to frighten him off.'

The cat yowled overhead once more, little more than a blur.

'Well he's certainly frightened, and he can't reach your flowerbeds from up there,' said Bronwen, trying not to smile. 'What was supposed to happen?'

Mrs Mortimer handed Bronwen a little paperback spell-book. 'That's the spell I meant to cast.'

'Call Up a Miniature Thunderstorm Over Your Neighbour's Tom Cat,' read Bronwen. 'What's he doing up there, then?'

'About 800 miles an hour!' chortled a boy

who was looking over the other fence. 'You can hear the crack as he goes through the sound barrier.'

'The wind blew the pages over while I was chanting the spell,' said Mrs Mortimer.

Bronwen looked at the two spells after the one that Mrs Mortimer had tried to cast. They were "Teach Your Toothbrush to Fly" and "Send a Snail Through the Sound Barrier".

'Can you get him down?' asked Mrs Mortimer.

'No, I'm afraid not . . .'

'What?' screamed Doey's owner. 'I'll have the RSPCA on you! My poor little Doey, doomed to spend the rest of his life . . .'

' . . . but you can, Mrs Mortimer,' finished Bronwen.

'Me?' exclaimed Mrs Mortimer.

'Yes, it's all in this book. All you have to do to reverse the spell is to say it backwards.'

'Oh dear, I didn't see that bit.' She took the book from Bronwen. 'Sound of speed . . .' she began to chant.

'No, that won't do,' said Bronwen. 'You

have to say the words backwards too.'

'Oh dear,' said Mrs Mortimer, unhappily peering at the spells. 'I can't. It's impossible.'

'You've got to!' said Bronwen. 'Unless you want to leave Doey up there for ever. It's not too difficult if you take it slowly.'

'Oh dear,' said Mrs Mortimer again, and slowly and hesitantly began reading the spell. 'Dnous fo deeps eht deexce dna.'

As she turned the page to the previous spell for the next line the cat, which until now had been little more than a blur and a yowl, suddenly became distinctly visible, zig-zagging over the gardens at a more leisurely pace. It was apparent now that the reason why he had not disappeared over the horizon was that his furiously lashing tail was acting as a rudder, constantly changing his course.

There was a small black cloud over him, within which could be seen tiny flashes of lightning. And to add to his discomfort, the cloud was pouring rain over him, and also over the neighbours as he darted hither and thither.

'My poor little Doey!' groaned his owner. 'What have you done to him?'

He certainly did look a bit odd. His front paws were scrabbling wildly in the air, as if he was trying to dig a hole in the air, and his back legs were tightly crossed. And he was still yowling piteously.

'He's not really hurt,' Bronwen assured her. 'Now Mrs Mortimer, chant the next line, but don't say the last word until he's over his own garden.'

'Dnuorg eht ffo teg, ylf tsum . . .'

She paused and watched as the caterwauling animal zig-zagged haphazardly to and fro. It was impossible to judge where he was going next. But suddenly, as he was about to crash into Mrs Mortimer's bedroom window, he abruptly changed direction and headed towards his own garden.

'Now!' cried Bronwen.

'Uoy!' cried Mrs Mortimer, furiously waving her wand.

Doey dropped like a stone. The yowling stopped and his legs shot out sideways, as if to try to slow his descent. But his hind legs

quickly snapped crossed again. His mistress rushed across her garden, arms outstretched, and just managed to catch him.

'There, there,' she said soothingly, clutching him tight and stroking his head. 'You're safe now. Mummy's got you.'

But Doey did not want to be got. He had more urgent things to attend to. He screeched and struggled and scratched himself free, and streaked across the lawn to the nearest flower-bed, where he started to dig frantically, plants and earth flying in all directions.

With a cry of rage, his mistress snatched up a broom and charged at him.

'You mangy, flea-bitten moggy!' she shrieked. 'How dare you dig up my garden! How many times do I have to tell you to do it somewhere else?'

She took a swipe at Doey, but he had seen her coming and, desperate though he was, he was already in flight on to and over Mrs Mortimer's fence. He landed in amongst Mrs Mortimer's seedlings, his front paws already digging frenziedly as he hit the ground, but Mrs Mortimer made no attempt to stop him.

'Poor thing!' she exclaimed as he squatted over the hole he had made, with a look of extreme relief on his face. 'No wonder he had his legs crossed.'

'Don't forget the rest of the spell,' warned Bronwen.

But Mrs Mortimer was watching gleefully as, to the fury of her neighbour, the tiny black cloud drifted over the neighbour's rotary clothes line, drenching her washing.

'Serves her right!' she said. '"Mummy's got you", indeed! No wonder he's always using my garden – he's not allowed to go in his own.'

She went over to the cat and stroked him. 'You can come here any time you like, Doey. In fact, I'll dig you a nice soft patch all of your own.'

'The rest of the spell!' hissed Bronwen, as the diminutive storm rumbled across the fence, heading straight for Mrs Mortimer.

'Oh!' squealed Mrs Mortimer, as she was suddenly deluged in tiny drops of rain.

Bronwen held the spell-book out to her and, glaring at the boy who was howling with laughter at her discomfort, Mrs Mortimer chanted, 'Rood txen morf yggom no tsuj, Ruop tsum niar, gninthgil . . .'

She paused and looked at the boy who, too late, realised why she was grinning, and looked up just in time to receive the full force of the pint-sized thunderstorm full in the face.

'Rednuht!' cried Mrs Mortimer triumphantly.

2 Fred Gets a Helping Hand

'Oww-wowww-wowwww!' screamed the siren, and the blue light flashed as the Superintendent sped after the car which was going much too fast in a 30-mph zone. But the driver did not seem to have noticed the policeman on his tail. Probably got his radio on full blast, thought the Super, and he isn't bothering to watch his rear-view mirror.

The car started to wink its left indicator, and the Super suddenly grinned impishly. He swerved off the road to the left and shot over a hedge. Instantly everything went white as he became enveloped in Mrs Mortimer's neighbour's sheets, which she was just hanging out again after spin-drying them for the second time that morning.

She sprang back in alarm as her rotary clothes line spun round at enormous speed, tripped, and sat down in her fish-pond. With the cold, slimy, green water slowly soaking her to the skin, she stared in disbelief as a policeman on a broomstick emerged from her washing, saluted, and raced off across the fence.

He zoomed across several more gardens and shot between two houses, to emerge just in front of the speeding car as it accelerated away from the junction. The Superintendent slewed round, and whizzed along backwards just above the car's bonnet, hand outstretched in a 'stop' gesture just centimetres from the startled driver's face.

The car almost stood on its nose as it screeched to a halt, and its driver stared white-faced with fright and pop-eyed with incredulity as the senior policeman on his broomstick floated down alongside the open window, taking a notebook from his pocket.

'Good morning, sir,' said the Superintendent politely. 'Now then, we're not red, are we, so we're not on our way to a fire. And we're not white, so we can't be going to the hospital, can we?'

The driver gulped, and shook his head.

'So what colour are we, sir?'

The driver leaned out of his window and peered down at the side of his car. 'Er, blue,' he said.

'Very observant, sir. Blue. Now where would something blue be going in a hurry? Let me think.'

The driver watched him apprehensively. 'Yes, of course!' exclaimed the Superintendent. 'Prison vans are blue.'

The driver went even whiter. 'Prison? But I was only speeding!'

'Ah, jolly good, a confession. I like a man who admits his crimes.' The Superintendent spoke into his radio. 'Superbroom to Cop-shop.'

'Yes, sir?' quacked the radio.

'Ah, Eddie, my boy. I have a gentleman here who is going to drive ever so slowly and carefully to the police station to confess his crimes. Look after him, won't you? I expect he'd like a cup of tea.'

PC Eddie Wagstaff passed the message to Sergeant Lennox, who was desk sergeant this week. 'I'm off on my beat again, then, Sarge,' he said, putting on his helmet.

Bronwen studied the recipe for Acne Ointment, which was still on the SpelComputer's screen, then selected the ingredients from the shelves above the bench.

She had still been chuckling when she got back from Mrs Mortimer, but had quickly lost her good mood when she learned from the broomsticks that the telephone had rung four times while she had been out, and that a lot of people had tried the door.

She sighed, wondering how many customers were lost for good, switched on her electric cauldron, and began to mix the potion. Then she sighed again in exasperation as the old-fashioned bell over the shop door jingle-jangled. She was *never* going to get this potion made up.

PC Wagstaff was in the shop. His mother was also a witch, although he had only found out about it a few days ago, soon after Bronwen had first opened her shop. He had almost arrested her for flight-testing a broomstick in the High Street.

'Hullo, Eddie,' said Bronwen. 'Not more problems with the Super, I hope?'

'Oh no,' smiled the young policeman. 'No more bad tempers now he has that potion in his tea every day. And he's having a whale of a time with the broomstick you gave him. It's you I'm worried about.'

'Me?' exclaimed Bronwen.

'Well, the shop was closed when I came by on my beat earlier.' He looked at her closely. 'And you don't look very well.'

'Just tired,' said Bronwen. 'The shop was closed because I was called out on an emergency.'

'The night shift say your lights are on late at night, and early in the morning, too,' said Wagstaff. 'No wonder you're tired. You shouldn't work so hard, Bronwen.'

Bronwen gestured towards the half-empty potion shelves behind the counter. 'It's the only way I can keep my potion stocks up, Eddie. It's hopeless trying to do it during the day. There are too many interruptions.'

'Why don't you get an assistant?'

'Oh, I've thought about it, Eddie, but I'm not sure I can afford to, yet. I still owe the bank an awful lot of money. And how do I know I could trust an assistant not to meddle with the spells and potions?'

'Well, you can't go on like this, Bronwen. Promise me you'll do something, even if you only get a telephone-answering machine.'

Bronwen smiled wanly. 'All right, Eddie. I promise. Would you like a cup of tea?'

'No, thanks,' said Wagstaff. 'I'd better be off. I want to finish my beat before the Super gets back and makes the tea.'

'The Superintendent makes tea for *you*?'

exclaimed Bronwen in surprise.

'Oh yes, he never bawls and shouts for me to make it any more, thanks to you. But I like to beat him to it, if I can, now I don't have to.'

When he had gone, Bronwen returned to the workroom and stared at the mixture in the cauldron in dismay. Once more, she had completely forgotten where she was up to.

Dejectedly she tipped the potion down the sink, washed the cauldron, and started again, chanting the spell as she dropped the ingredients into the cauldron. This particular spell could be sung, if you wished, but Bronwen was in no mood for singing.

'Half a glug of Steamroller Squash,' she chanted, tipping in the thick, murky, evil-smelling and very heavy liquid.

'Sandpaper gone rotten'.

It had to be rotten, because fresh sandpaper will not dissolve.

'That's the way to get Acne down,
Smooth as a baby's bottom.'

She added the water, turned on the stirring blades and started the timer. But only just in time, because the bell jingle-jangled again.

She served a customer with a tube of Teething Trouble Paste for his new car, then sat on the stool behind the counter, wondering how she could keep her promise to Eddie. An answering machine would certainly solve part of the problem, although she knew that some people do not like talking to them, but it could not deal with the customers who came to the door.

'I'm a witch!' she exclaimed out loud. 'I sort out other people's problems, why can't I solve my own?'

There was a sudden silence from the broomsticks, but as soon as they realised that she was not talking to them they resumed their incessant chatter, which quickly rose to a crescendo.

'Shush, broomsticks!' said Bronwen. 'I can't hear myself think.'

There was a brief silence, then they all started talking again, although a little more quietly.

'Miss!' said one of them, after a while.

Bronwen was deep in thought, and did not reply.

'Miss!'

Bronwen looked up. 'Yes?'

'Miss, are we still making too much noise?'

'No, it's all right now, thank you,' said Bronwen.

'Well, I can't hear you thinking. Have you stopped?'

Bronwen smiled. 'I don't *really* think out loud,' she said. '"Can't hear myself think" is just an expression.'

The broomstick looked puzzled. 'What's an expression, miss?'

'It's a phrase that doesn't mean what it seems to mean.'

'Oh,' said the broomstick. 'What's a phrase?'

'Oh dear,' sighed Bronwen, wishing she had never started this conversation. 'Well, it's a sort of sentence.'

She was relieved when the broomstick did not pursue the matter but, still looking puzzled, went back to talking to its friends. But the inquisitiveness of the broomstick had given her an idea. It was obviously eager to learn, even though most broomsticks are not very bright.

'Broomstick,' she said.

The chattering stopped, and fourteen little faces turned towards her.

'You,' she said. 'The one who was talking to me. Come over here.'

It floated over to the counter, looking

worried, while the other broomsticks smirked at each other.

'I wasn't the only one talking!' protested the broomstick.

'I know,' said Bronwen, smiling at it to show she was not cross. 'And I want you to talk. I want you to answer the phone for me in future.'

The broomstick's little face beamed with delight, while the other broomsticks looked at each other in dismay.

'It's not fair!' one of them muttered, loud enough for Bronwen to hear.

'Witch's pet!' said another.

'Let's try it,' said Bronwen. 'Pretend the phone is ringing and pick it up.'

The broomstick's face dropped. 'I-I can't,' it whispered unhappily.

'Nonsense!' said Bronwen. 'It's nothing to be afraid of!'

'No, miss, but . . .'

'Then do it!'

'I *can't,* miss!'

'Why on earth not?' snapped Bronwen impatiently.

'I–I've got nothing to pick it up *with*!' wailed the broomstick.

'He's quite 'armless, miss,' called a broomstick.

'You'll have to give him a hand!' giggled another.

'Or the elbow!' snorted a third.

'And so I shall!' retorted Bronwen. 'And you'd better have a name, too.'

She came out from behind the counter and led the frightened broomstick into the treatment room, closing the door behind her. She plugged in the electric wand and began to chant a spell in the dirgelike tone she had been taught at college.

'Digits sprout,
Elbows form,
Limbs develop,
Appendages born.'

'I hereby dub you Fred,' she said solemnly, tapping him with the wand where his shoulders would be, if broomsticks had shoulders. Fred recoiled, and cried out with fear as tiny sparks flew.

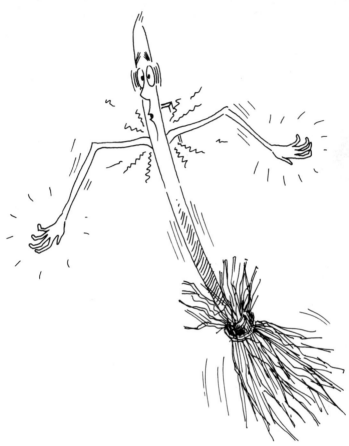

'There, Fred,' said Bronwen a few seconds
later. '*Now* you can use the phone.'

Fred held his new hands up to his face and
slowly wiggled his new fingers, gazing at
them in wonder.

'Come on!' smiled Bronwen. 'Come outside and try them out.'

3 Fred Helps Himself

The other broomsticks stared in astonishment at Fred when he and Bronwen came out of the treatment room hand in hand. Bronwen led Fred over to the telephone.

'Try picking it up, Fred,' she said.

Fred slowly reached out for the phone, but just as his hand touched it, it rang. He leapt back in alarm.

'Go on, Fred!' laughed Bronwen. 'Answer it. Say, "Witches' Cauldron, can I help you?"'

Fred gave her a quick, nervous, little smile then, looking very apprehensive, floated over to the phone again and picked it up.

'Witches' Cauldron, can I help you?' he whispered, as if he was afraid that the person at the other end would hear him.

Then he looked puzzled. 'There's no-one there!' he said.

Bronwen laughed again and gently turned

the phone around, so that Fred was no longer listening to the mouthpiece. 'Say I'm out, find out who it is and what they want, and say I'll ring back,' she whispered.

'Well?' she said, when Fred finally put the phone down.

'It was Mr Wagstaff, and he said . . .' Fred frowned with concentration. 'He said he wants a small Aero and a box of maggots and his voice sounded a bit funny.'

'Oh Fred!' exclaimed Bronwen. 'That can't be right! Oh dear, if you can't remember one message five seconds after you've been given it, how are you going to manage when I'm out for a long time? You'd better write everything down, and read it back to the caller to make sure you've got it right.'

She was surprised to see tears starting to run down Fred's handle.

'Whatever's the matter?' she asked. 'I'm not cross with you, Fred.'

'I'm useless!' snuffled Fred. 'Now you'll take my arms away again.'

'Of course I won't. How can you write without arms?'

'I can't write *with* them!' Fred sobbed. 'I don't know how to!'

Of course! thought Bronwen. It's me that's stupid. Broomsticks don't normally have arms, so their brains aren't programmed to be able to write.

'I'm sorry, Fred,' she apologised. 'It's my fault. I should have realised. Don't worry – when the lunchtime rush is over, we'll go out and buy something to help you. Now let's find out what Eddie really wants.'

PC Wagstaff laughed when Bronwen rang him up to ask what message he had given Fred. 'But it wasn't me, Bronwen,' he said. 'This new assistant of yours had got that wrong, too. Could it have been Mother?'

'Fred did say your voice sounded a bit funny, but I thought that was because he hadn't used a phone before. I'll ask her.'

Mrs Wagstaff said it had been her, and she laughed too when she heard what Fred had told Bronwen she wanted. 'I suppose it's nearly right,' she chuckled. 'But what I *really* want is a small aerosol of Burp of Maggot. I asked your assistant to give it to Eddie, when he comes into the shop next. Perhaps that's what confused him.'

After the lunchtime rush, Bronwen's busiest time of day, when she never went out or tried to make up potions, she locked the shop and took Fred out into the High Street. She strode down the High Street, with a very excited Fred at her side. He tried hard to swing his arms like a human, but ended up swinging them backwards and forwards together, to the alarm of passers-by, who thought he was about to jump on them. They went into the police station to give Wagstaff the potion.

'What a marvellous idea!' exclaimed Wagstaff, when Bronwen introduced Fred to him, and to the Superintendent and the other policemen. 'Perhaps he could run errands for you, too, or fly them, anyway!'

On the way back up the High Street Bronwen bought a small cassette recorder, with a gadget to attach it to the telephone, so that every message Fred took would be recorded. Then, just before they reached 'The Witches'

Cauldron', she turned down a side street and went into a snack bar.

'Hullo, Bronwen,' said the girl behind the counter, staring rather uncertainly at Fred. 'What would you like today?'

'I'll have an egg salad, please, Julie,' said Bronwen. 'And this is Fred. He'll be coming to get my lunch in future, so that I don't have to leave the shop.'

'Pleased to meet you, Fred,' said Julie, putting the cling-film-wrapped salad on the counter. 'He certainly doesn't need to slim, does he? Is there anything else?'

'Yes, a strawberry ice-cream, please,' said Bronwen.

Julie scooped the ice-cream into a cone. 'Is this for Fred?'

Fred's eyes lit up, and he started to hold out his hand.

'Oh no!' laughed Bronwen, taking the cone. 'That's for me. Broomsticks don't eat!'

'No wonder he's thin,' grinned Julie.

Bronwen paid Julie, gave the salad to Fred to carry, and walked out licking her ice-cream. She soon became aware that Fred was

gazing up at her, looking very woebegone.

'What's the matter, Fred?'

'I would have liked to *try* an ice-cream,' he said dolefully.

'But Fred, broomsticks don't eat!'

But he looked so mournful that she gave in. 'All right, I don't suppose it can do any harm. Just a taste, mind.'

A grin spread across Fred's little face, and he took a big slurp of the ice-cream. 'Ooh, that's . . .!' he paused. 'I don't know any words for something that tastes nice.'

'"Delicious" is a good word to describe ice-cream,' suggested Bronwen.

'Delicious!' repeated Fred enthusiastically, licking ice-cream from around his lips. 'Delicious, delicious, delicious!'

'Well, don't tell the others,' said Bronwen, unlocking the door of the shop. 'Or they'll all want a lick, and they're jealous enough of you already.'

She attached the recorder to the telephone and showed Fred how to turn it on and off, and left him to answer any calls while she had her lunch in peace, interrupted only by people who came into the shop.

The afternoon was much more peaceful than usual. Fred took all the telephone calls, and Bronwen was able to play them back and deal with them whenever it was convenient, instead of having to stop whatever she was doing every time the phone rang. When she closed the shop that evening she had far less work left to do, and she would not have to come in nearly so early in the morning, either. She was very pleased with her idea.

The next day she showed Fred how to lock and unlock the door, so that he could ask any customer who came while she was out to write a message on a notepad, or he would tell them when to come back, if they would rather.

The system worked well. Bronwen now knew who had telephoned or who had called in while she was out, and what they wanted. And if she was in, but was in the middle of making up a potion, Fred would either take the telephone call or, if someone came into the shop, he would ask them to wait. And he came back with her lunch bursting with pride at being trusted to go out on his own.

But on the third day, when she had closed for the night and was counting the money in the till, she discovered that she was a few pounds short. She checked again and again, but to no avail. She must have given someone too much change. Unless . . .

'Fred, has anyone been in the shop today, while I was out?'

'No, miss. I make them stand in the doorway to write their messages.'

'So no-one's been anywhere near the till?'

'No, miss.'

'If they did, we'd hit them,' declared a broomstick from the rack.

'And beat them and bash them!' cried another broomstick gleefully.

'And biff them and thump them!'

'And slosh them and wallop them!'

'And clout them and clobber them!'

'And slap them and smack them!'

'All right, all right, I believe you!' said Bronwen.

It was true, it was impossible for anyone to steal anything from the shop while Bronwen was out, day or night, for the broomsticks were automatically spellbound to act as security guards. And anyway, why would anyone take just a little money, and not all of it? She must have made a mistake with someone's change.

But when the same thing happened the following day, too, Bronwen knew she couldn't possibly have made the same mistake again. Not for exactly the same amount.

'Fred, there *must* have been someone in here today. And yesterday.'

'No, miss, there hasn't,' insisted Fred. 'Has there?'

'Definitely not,' agreed one of the broomsticks in the rack, while the rest shook their handles in agreement.

'Then *where* has the money gone?' asked Bronwen rather crossly.

There was a sudden silence, and Bronwen noticed that all the broomsticks were looking at Fred.

'Did *you* steal it, Fred?'

Fred gulped and looked frightened. 'Wh-what does "steal" mean, miss?'

'It's what burglars do, taking something that doesn't belong to them. That's why you're supposed to biff them and bash them.'

'Oh, that's all right then,' said Fred, looking very relieved.

'What's all right?'

'I'm not a burglar, so I didn't steal it.'

Bronwen stared at him. 'But you *do* know what happened to it.'

'Oh yes, miss,' said Fred brightly.

Bronwen put her face close to Fred's. '*What* happened to it? And what's that mess around your mouth?'

'Ice-cream,' grinned Fred.

'Ice-cream?' repeated Bronwen. 'You took the money to buy an ice-cream?'

'Yes.'

'But an ice-cream wouldn't have cost all that money!'

'One *each*,' explained Fred.

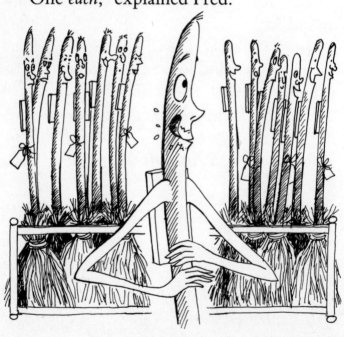

'They were delicious!' chorused the two rows of new broomsticks.

'He had a lick of everyone else's,' complained a voice from the rack of secondhand broomsticks in the workroom.

'And you don't call that stealing?' demanded Bronwen.

'Of course not,' said Fred. 'You said burglars steal, and I'm not a burglar. Anyway, it was me who went out and got them, and held them so that they could lick them, so I think I'm entitled to a lick of everyone else's.'

'I meant the *money*!' exclaimed Bronwen. 'Taking it from the till is stealing, whether you're a burglar or not!'

'*You* take money from the till!' protested Fred.

'But it's *my* money!' said Bronwen. 'And I take it to the bank.'

'There, you see!' cried Fred triumphantly. 'I buy ice-creams and you buy banks. That's fair, isn't it? What's a bank? Is it delicious?'

'What's a bank?' snapped Bronwen. 'A bank's . . .'

She suddenly giggled. She tried to become cross again, but it was no good. They were like little children, they just did not understand that they had done anything wrong. And it was no wonder that all the broomsticks were friends with Fred again, with him feeding them ice-cream every day. The crawler!

'All right, Fred,' she said. 'I'll let you off this time. But you must never ever do it again. You must only do what you're told to do, nothing else. Do you understand?'

Fred nodded dejectedly. Bronwen got a damp cloth from the sink in the workroom and wiped the dried ice-cream from their faces. She was dealing with the secondhand broomsticks in the workroom when the phone rang.

'Answer it, Fred!' she called. 'Tell them I'm not in.'

4   *Taken into Custody*

Bronwen heard the click as Fred switched the recorder on, then he picked up the phone.

'Witches' Cauldron, can I help you?'

Then, to Bronwen's consternation, he went on, 'Miss Smith says she's not in . . . Yes, she's here, but she's not in, can I . . .?

Bronwen grabbed the phone from him. 'You mustn't say *that*!' she hissed.

'But you said . . .!'

'Can I help you?' asked Bronwen, ignoring his protest.

'Bronwen, thank goodness you're there!' cried Wagstaff.

'What's the matter, Eddie?'

'It's the Super again, Bronwen. He's going berserk!'

'Isn't the potion working?'

'It was his day off yesterday, so I couldn't give it to him.'

'Well, that wouldn't matter if you put some in his tea first thing this morning,' said Bronwen.

'He was all right this morning, apart from a sore throat, so I just didn't think of it.'

'Do it now, then. He hasn't gone off tea, has he?'

'No, of course not. He's screaming for tea, tea and more tea. It's just that . . .'

'What, Eddie?'

'Well, I've lost the potion.'

'I thought you kept it in the station first-aid cupboard.'

'I do, Bronwen. I'm sure I put it back after I gave him his dose the day before yesterday, but it's gone. I've asked everyone here, except the Super, of course, but no-one's seen it.'

'Where's my tea?' bellowed a voice in the background.

'No wonder he's got a sore throat,' chuckled Bronwen, picturing the Superintendent's red, angry face.

'It's not funny, Bronwen,' muttered Wagstaff.

'No. Sorry, Eddie,' said Bronwen, glad he

couldn't see the grin on her face.

'Wagstaff, where's my tea?' roared a voice in Bronwen's ear.

'I'm on the phone, sir!' hissed Wagstaff.

'I don't care if you're on fire!' bawled the Superintendent. 'Get me some more tea before I get cross!'

'I'll have to go, Bronwen,' said Wagstaff. 'Be as quick as you can, won't you?'

'Are you talking to that ghastly Smith woman?' cried the Superintendent. 'Cooking up more mischief, I'll be bound!'

'But you like Bronwen, sir,' protested Wagstaff. 'She gave you your broomstick, remember? You have a lot of fun with that.'

'Broomsticks? Fiddlesticks! There's no such thing! Now stop nattering to that awful woman and get my tea! What do you think you're in the police force for?'

He strode into his office and slammed the door behind him.

'Sorry, Bronwen,' said Wagstaff.

'All right, Eddie. Don't worry. I'll be round in a few minutes with some more potion.'

'Oh, there's no need to come yourself, Bronwen. Why don't you send Fred? I know how busy you are.'

'That's a good idea. All right, I will.'

She quickly made up several bottles of the potion which Wagstaff added to the Superintendent's tea every day, to cure his dreadful temper, and handed one to Fred.

'Now remember,' warned Bronwen. 'You do *exactly* as you're told, and nothing else. Straight there, and straight back, understand?'

'Yes, miss,' said Fred, very proud of being sent on his first errand, apart from getting Bronwen's lunch.

'Right, off you go.'

She opened the door to let him out, and he smirked self-importantly at the other broomsticks before speeding off down the High Street.

PC Wagstaff poured tea from the big teapot into a mug and knocked on the door of the Superintendent's office.

'If that's my tea, you can come in!' bellowed the Superintendent. 'If not, go away!'

Wagstaff nervously opened the door and went in. He placed the mug in front of the Superintendent, grabbed the empty mug and retreated hurriedly. A distinguished-looking man in uniform was standing at the

counter. Wagstaff stared at him in horror.

'Evening, constable,' said the man. 'I've come to see the Superintendent.'

Wagstaff shot a worried look towards the office door. 'Well, he's a bit tied up at the moment, sir,' he said nervously.

'Tied up? In his own police station? Are you in the middle of a robbery, then?' chuckled the man.

Wagstaff gave a sickly sort of smile. 'N-no, sir. You know what I mean.'

'No, I don't!' snapped the man. 'Do you know who I am?'

'Th-the Chief Constable, sir.'

'And what is the Superintendent doing that he can't see his own boss? Especially since he asked me to come.'

'Well, it's just that . . .' Wagstaff trailed off miserably.

The Chief Constable glared at him and strode behind the counter and past the petrified Wagstaff.

'You're trying to cover something up!' he cried. 'I'm going to get to the bottom of this!'

He threw open the office door and slammed it closed behind him, to a roar of rage from the Superintendent.

'Mr Wagstaff,' came a voice from behind Wagstaff, almost drowned by the thunderous argument in the office.

'Oh, thank goodness you're here, Fred,' said Wagstaff, turning and taking the bottle of potion from the broomstick's hand.

The office door burst open and the Superintendent came out, holding the Chief Constable's arm in a half-nelson.

'Wagstaff, arrest this man!'

Wagstaff's eyes widened. 'Arrest him, sir?'

'Yes, arrest him!'

'But sir, he's the Chief Constable!'

'I don't care if he's the Chief Bridesmaid. The law's the same for him as for anyone else. Arrest him!'

'Yes, sir. What shall I charge him with?'

'Interruption.'

'Interruption, sir?'

'Don't keep repeating everything I say, Wagstaff!'

'But interrupting isn't a criminal offence, sir.'

'Of course it is!' snapped the Superintendent. 'Interrupting a police officer in the course of drinking his tea is a very serious offence.'

'Really, Superintendent, this has gone too far!' barked the Chief Constable. 'Let go of my arm!'

'Certainly, sir,' said the Superintendent. 'Wagstaff, handcuff him!'

'Handcuff . . .?'

'Wagstaff, you're doing it again. Do as you're told!'

Wagstaff looked unhappily from one senior police officer to the other, then snapped his handcuffs on to the Chief Constable's wrists.

'Sorry, sir,' he muttered to the Chief Constable.

'This is outrageous!' roared the Chief Constable.

'It certainly is!' retorted the Superintendent. 'How dare you come into my office when I'm drinking my tea? You wouldn't dream of doing so, would you Wagstaff?'

Wagstaff shook his head. 'No, sir.'

Which was perfectly true, with the Superintendent in his present mood.

'You see, Wagstaff knows it's illegal. I suppose you think you can get away with anything just because you're the Chief Constable. Well, not on my patch you can't!'

'Er, sir,' said Wagstaff. 'What do I do with the, er, prisoner now?'

'Do with him? Take him down to the cells, of course!'

Then he noticed Fred, who had been watching all this with great interest.

'You! Take the prisoner down!'

'But sir,' protested Wagstaff. 'He's not a . . .'

'Don't keep arguing, Wagstaff!'

'But I really think it would be better if I took the prisoner down to the cells, sir.'

'I've got something more important for you to do.' The Superintendent hustled the Chief Constable out from behind the counter and thrust him towards Fred. 'Take him down, and if he resists, hit him!'

Fred grinned. He couldn't wait to tell the other broomsticks how he had helped to arrest a dangerous criminal. Wouldn't they be jealous! But the Chief Constable stared at Fred in amazement, then laughed.

'It's a broomstick! Now I know you're playing a practical joke on me!'

'Broomstick?' The Superintendent's eyes narrowed. 'So you're in on this stupid broomstick joke, are you? Well, you can't fool me! There's no such thing as broomsticks! Take him down!'

Fred took the Chief Constable's elbow, but the Chief Constable did not move. He grinned.

'I don't know how you do it, Superintendent, but it's a marvellous joke. This broomstick gadget's incredible. Is it remote-controlled?' He held the handcuffs out to Wagstaff. 'I think the joke's gone far enough, though. Take these off, there's a good chap . . . OWW!'

Fred had cracked him over the head with his handle. He pushed the dazed and bewildered Chief Constable towards the stairs leading down to the cells.

'Hold him in custody until I say otherwise,' ordered the Superintendent. 'And go to the canteen while you're down there. You're far too thin for a policeman.'

The Chief Constable tried to protest again, but quickly changed his mind and stumbled down the stairs when Fred cracked him on the head again.

The Superintendent scowled after him, then turned and strode back towards his office.

'Excuse me, sir,' said Wagstaff. 'You had something important for me to do?'

'Yes, make a fresh pot of tea, of course.'

'Tea, sir?'

'Wagstaff!' growled the Superintendent warningly.

He went into his office and slammed the door. Wagstaff picked up the teapot and emptied the dregs down the sink, then switched on the electric kettle. He spooned tea into the pot, then looked at the bottle of potion that he still had in his hand and smiled.

'Wagstaff, hurry up with that tea!'

5 A Sticky Problem (or Two)

Bronwen finished making up another potion, then looked at her watch. 'Is Fred back yet?' she called.

'No, miss!' chorused the broomsticks, out in the shop.

Bronwen frowned. 'That's funny,' she muttered to herself. 'He should be back by now. I hope he's not getting into mischief again.'

She picked up the phone and dialled the police station. 'Eddie, is Fred still there?'

'Oh, yes, sorry Bronwen. I'd forgotten about him. He's down in the cells.'

'In the cells? Have you arrested him?'

'No, but we have arrested the Chief Constable.'

'Arrested the Chief Constable? What on earth for?'

'Interrupting the Super while he was drinking his tea.'

'What are you talking about, Eddie? Is this a joke?'

'That's what the Chief Constable thought, until Fred hit him on the head.'

'Oh, no!' cried Bronwen. 'Then you have arrested Fred?'

Wagstaff sighed. 'No, Fred was arresting the Chief Constable at the time. The Super told him to. Look, it's awfully complicated, Bronwen. I think it would be best if I just send Fred back. Just a minute.'

He put the phone down and went over to the top of the stairs leading down to the cells. 'Fred!' he shouted.

'Yes, Mr Wagstaff?' came back a faint voice.

'You've got to go back to the shop now!'

'But what about the criminal? The Superintendent said I've got to hold him in . . .'

'Just make sure the cell door's locked, and bring the key up to me,' ordered Wagstaff.

There was a dull thud, accompanied by an anguished cry and the sound of a cell door being slammed and locked. Wagstaff sighed again and returned to the phone.

'Here he comes now, Bronwen,' he said, as Fred floated up the stairs. 'I'll send him straight back.'

'Are you speaking to Bronwen, Eddie?' said a voice behind him. 'Excuse me.' The Superintendent beamed at Wagstaff and took the phone from Wagstaff's unresisting fingers. 'Hullo, my dear,' he said. 'Have you got a moment to pop round? The Chief Constable's here, and I want you to meet him. I'm going to try to persuade him to replace our cars with broomsticks. They're jolly good for catching villains. You'll be right round. Jolly good! I'll put the kettle on!'

'Such a nice young lady,' he said to Wagstaff as he put the phone down. 'Now, where's the Chief Constable? I asked him to come here this evening, and I'm sure I heard his voice.'

'He's, er, in the cells, sir,' said Wagstaff apprehensively.

'Inspecting the cells, eh? Well, there's nothing wrong with our cells. They're all nice and warm and comfortable. Full, too. Don't forget to give the prisoners their hot-water bottles later, will you?'

'He's not exactly inspecting them, sir. More sort of, well, locked in one.'

'Locked in one? Has some fool arrested him?'

'Well, er, yes they have, sir.'

'Whatever for?'

'Interrupting you while you were drinking your tea.'

The Superintendent grinned. 'You must

be kidding me, Eddie. It's not April Fool's Day, is it?'

'No, sir. I'm perfectly serious.'

'You *are* pulling my leg! You wouldn't *dare* arrest the Chief Constable, even if he had done something wrong, and even if I told you myself to arrest him.'

'Me?' spluttered Wagstaff indignantly. 'I assure you sir, the Chief Constable is locked in a cell, and he is not laughing. He is very cross, in fact. And it wasn't *my* idea to . . .'

'Oh dear, Eddie, what have you done? You should never have tried to play a practical joke on him. The man has no sense of humour,' said the Superintendent. 'We'd better let him out and butter him up a bit. Is there plenty of tea brewed?'

'Yes, sir.'

'Good. A nice cup of tea will soon calm him down. Pouring tea on troubled Chief Constables, eh, Eddie?' He chuckled at his own joke. 'We'll soon get you out of trouble.'

'Fred, go and let the Chief Constable out

of his cell,' said Wagstaff, angrily thrusting his hands into his pockets. At least the Chief Constable knew who was *really* responsible for his arrest. His fingers encountered the bottle of potion, and he sighed with relief. A nice cup of tea *would* put the Chief Constable in a good mood.

'I say, that's a jolly good idea!' exclaimed the Superintendent, as Fred swept back down the stairs, jingling his keys. 'Having a broomstick for a warder. Jolly useful things, broomsticks. Must suggest that to the Chief Constable, too. I'm sure he'll agree.'

There was a loud crash from downstairs as a cell door burst open, and heavy footsteps sounded on the stairs.

'Where's that clodhopping flatfoot?' thundered the Chief Constable.

He arrived at the top of the stairs like an enraged bull, red-faced, eyes popping, hair dishevelled and strange yellow splodges on his once immaculate uniform. His eyebrows almost joined up with his moustache as his bloodshot eyes fixed on the Superintendent.

'Imbecile! Blockhead! Scatterwit!' he

screamed. 'You're not fit to superintend a teddy bears' picnic!'

'I'm sure Wagstaff only meant it as a joke,' the Superintendent said.

'A joke? You ordering that – that broomstick to hit me was a *joke*? And do you know what this is?'

He scooped a yellow blob from his arm and smeared it on the Superintendent's uniform. The Superintendent took a little on his finger, smelled it, then tentatively licked it.

'It's custard,' he said.

'I *know* it's custard!'

Wagstaff had at last been able to drag his attention away from the Chief Constable's apoplectic face, and was inspecting the rest of this strange apparition. The Chief Constable's shoes and the bottom of his trouser-legs were soaked in the yellow slime.

'Have you been standing in it, sir?' he asked incredulously.

'Of course not!' snapped the Chief Constable sarcastically. 'I always eat custard with my feet!'

'Well, I don't think it's very nice of you to

blame us if you get in a mess, then,' said the Superintendent. 'I mean, how can you hold the spoon properly with your shoes on? You're bound to get it all over you.'

The Chief Constable's eyes looked as if they were about to pop out of his head and ping across the room, and his lips curled in a fearsome grimace. He scooped great dollops of custard from his slimy tunic and leapt at the Superintendent, rubbing it in his hair, pushing it down inside his collar and laughing hysterically.

The laughing stopped abruptly as Fred appeared up the stairs and cracked the Chief Constable over the head again. The Chief Constable slumped to the floor, dazed.

The Superintendent looked at him aghast, hurried over to the teapot and started pouring mugs of tea.

'Fred, stop it!' cried Bronwen, who had just arrived, and had seen Fred hit the Chief Constable. She looked at the custard, which was splattered everywhere, and at the man lying on the floor. 'Who is he, and why are you hitting him?'

'He's a dangerous criminal called Chief Constable,' said Fred. 'I hit him because he was attacking the Superintendent.'

'And what's all this mess?'

'Custard,' said Fred. 'It's his own fault he got it all over himself. He wouldn't stand still in it until I'd hit him a few times. He kept jumping up and down in it.'

'What are you talking about? Why was the Chief Constable standing in custard in the first place?'

'Because the Superintendent told me to get some from the canteen downstairs and hold him in it, of course.'

Wagstaff, who had been listening to all this open-mouthed, suddenly realised what had happened. '*Custody*, not custard, Fred! He just meant you to lock him in.'

'Oh,' said Fred, looking a little crestfallen. 'Have I made a mess of it?'

'You certainly have,' sighed Wagstaff. 'In more ways than one.'

'Well,' said Fred, brightening up. 'I'm sure I've got the next bit right. We've got to butter him up, haven't we?'

'We certainly have . . . No, Fred!'

But it was too late. They had not noticed
that Fred had been carrying something in his
hand, and he was now smearing it all over

the Chief Constable, all yellow and greasy.

'There!' cried Fred. 'Now I'll get some tea to pour . . .'

He clattered lifelessly to the floor. Bronwen relaxed the wide-eyed stare with which she had removed all Fred's spell-power, and looked sadly at Wagstaff.

'I'm sorry,' she said dejectedly.

Wagstaff put a consoling arm around her shoulders. 'Oh, it's not your fault, Bronwen. It's mine, for losing the potion.'

Bronwen looked down at the broomstick lying on the floor, his eyes closed, his arms gone. 'Poor Fred,' she said. 'I suppose I expected too much of him.'

'Is he dead?' asked Wagstaff.

'No, he'll be all right when I give him back his spell-power. But I won't use him as an assistant again. Broomsticks just aren't bright enough.'

'Would he like a cup of tea?' asked the Superintendent, who was carrying four mugs.

'No, thank you,' said Bronwen, with a little smile.

'Is one of those for the Chief Constable, sir?' asked Wagstaff.

'Yes, it'll make him feel better.'

Wagstaff shook a few drops of potion into one of the mugs.

'What's that?' asked the Superintendent.

'Some medicine to make him feel even betterer,' said Wagstaff.

'Ah, that reminds me,' said the Superintendent. 'I must take a dose of the medicine I found in the first aid cupboard this morning. It sounds like just the thing for a sore throat.'

Wagstaff stared at him. 'Medicine?' he whispered.

'Yes. "Super Soothing Syrup" it says on the label,' said the Superintendent, taking the missing bottle of potion from his pocket and taking a swig. He chuckled. 'With a name like that, it might have been made specially for me!'

6 Sally Stirs up Trouble

But although Bronwen dared not use a broomstick as an assistant again, the few days when she had had Fred to help her had convinced her that she really did need aid.

There were many applicants for the job. Some of them thought they would be working in a joke shop, but it was still very difficult for Bronwen to decide which of the others was the most suitable. But she finally made her choice, and the following Monday morning found Sally already waiting in the shop doorway when she arrived.

'Hullo, Sally,' said Bronwen. 'You're nice and early.'

'Good morning, Miss Smith,' said Sally, rather shyly. She had just left school, and this was her first job. She was rather nervous, although Bronwen was not that much older, having only left Witches' Training College recently herself.

'Call me Bronwen,' said Bronwen, as she unlocked the door and led Sally inside. 'Miss Smith hasn't really got a witch sound to it, has it?'

She showed Sally where to hang her coat, in the workroom at the rear of the shop, and gave her a white coat to wear. Then she pointed to the rows of jars, bottles and boxes on the shelves above the workbench.

'Those are all ingredients for the potions,' she explained. 'You must never, on any account, open any of them. It could be very dangerous. Just imagine this is a chemist's shop. You wouldn't dream of making up the medicines, would you?'

Sally shook her head. 'No, Miss . . . Bronwen, I mean.'

'And you mustn't touch that,' said Bronwen, pointing to the cauldron. 'Or meddle with the computer. You must never, *ever* attempt to make up potions or cast spells.'

In the shop she showed Sally where everything was. 'Complete Home Witch' outfits in plastic-sealed boxes, rows of plastic bats, cats and ravens, and various types of

spell-books, from cheap paperbacks to expensive leather-bound volumes, filled the shelves.

There were SpelComputers, a rack of programmes for ordinary computers, and a whole range of cauldrons, from miniature versions (to go on a cooker ring) up to full-size ones, electric ones and the most up-to-date microwave cauldrons.

Behind the counter there were rows and

rows of boxes and bottles with silver labels, containing ready-made potions. Sally peered at some of the labels. Knock-Knee Repellent, Pin-Back-Your-Ears-Cream, Strawberry-flavoured Boomerang Jam for straying tortoises and Straight-forward Oil of Crow for Round-the-Bend Supermarket Trolleys.

Higher up were raw ingredients, for witches who wanted to make up their own potions, Chicken Clucks, Tail of Guinea-pig, Squeak of Rusty Hinge, Dewdrops from Cold Noses and many more. Sally would have loved to see what these mysterious things looked like.

'Never open any of them, Sally,' said Bronwen, as if reading her thoughts.

'Yes, Mi . . . Bronwen. But . . . guinea-pigs don't have tails.'

'No, not when you see them,' smiled Bronwen mysteriously, and she introduced Sally to the broomsticks, including Fred, who was back in the rack and feeling very disconsolate, to the delight of the other broomsticks.

Sally quickly settled down, and did her job well. Bronwen was very pleased with her. Sales went up, because there was always someone in the shop to serve customers, and Sally made careful notes of all the phone calls she took while Bronwen was out.

The following Tuesday, soon after the shop had opened, Bronwen's father rang up to say that her mother was not very well, and he wondered if Bronwen could possibly come and spend the day with her.

Tuesday was not a busy day for any of the shops in the town, so Bronwen agreed, and took off from the service road behind the shop on her broomstick.

Sally had very little to do all morning. She sold a few of the more common potions, and a 'Complete Home Witch' outfit to a woman who was shopping early for Christmas. So early, she's more like late for the last one, thought Sally. Several people phoned for Bronwen's advice or assistance, and Sally dutifully noted them down in the book, for Bronwen to deal with when she came back.

But otherwise she was rather bored. She dusted the shop and tidied up the potions and ingredients, then decided that Bronwen might be pleased if she checked the stock and made a note of everything she thought was getting a bit low.

Loose-Knicker-Elastic Drops was the only thing that really worried her. There was probably not enough to last the day, and Sally remembered that Bronwen had intended to make some up this morning. There were only three bottles left, and there was more than half the day to go.

Worried, Sally wandered into the workroom and gazed up at the rows of ingredients. It would be so easy to make up some more, if only Bronwen would let her. It was not as if she would have to use any of the stranger-sounding ingredients. All the ingredients for that particular spell were quite ordinary things, as far as potion ingredients go, anyway.

Sally went back into the shop and sat on her stool behind the counter. She looked around the shop, but could not think of a single thing more that she could do to occupy herself. She opened the till, but there was not much in there. And there would not be much more when Bronwen returned, if she did not have what the customers wanted.

Surely she could do no harm by mixing up some more potion. It was just like cooking, really. Just a matter of dropping a few things into the cauldron, not forgetting to chant the spell at the same time, of course. Sally giggled, and wondered if Bronwen chanted when she boiled an egg.

Her mind made up, Sally jumped from the stool and went back into the workroom. She did not even need to use the computer. She thumbed through the dog-eared spell-book that Bronwen used for the common potions until she came to the recipe, then carefully selected the ingredients from the shelf and placed the containers on the bench.

'For each litre of water used, add the following quantities in the order listed, while reciting the appropriate spell,' the instructions began. It said 'appropriate spell' because there was a slightly different spell for

Falling Sock Pick-Me-Up, although the recipe was the same.

Sally propped the spell-book up by the cauldron, with the open ingredient containers beside it, and dipped her hand into the first container. Drawing out six small round discs, she dropped them into the cauldron, chanting as she did so.

'Spots of Toadstool in the pot'.

Then she took a spoon and dug a teaspoonful of red, jam-like substance from a jar and tipped that in.

'London Bus to make it clot'.

Finally Sally distastefully put her finger

and thumb into a jar and took out a pinch of grey powder, and composed her face as the recipe directed the reader to do.

'Sprinkle Ghoulash with a frown,
Knickers will no more slip down.'

That was it. Nothing to it. All that remained was to add a litre of water and boil it for the correct time. She lowered the stirring paddles and switched on.

Jingle-jangle.

She had finished just in time. She left the potion to boil and went through into the shop. The customer was Mrs Venables. Sally had met her already. She was a witch from a nearby village, and she came in once a week, after she had done her shopping in the supermarket. Last week she had accidentally given Sally her grocery list by mistake, which rather confused Sally because she had not been able to find any of the things on the shelves. But Mrs Venables got it right this week, and gave Sally quite a long list of ingredients.

'I'm so glad Bronwen opened this shop,' she said, as Sally piled boxes, jars and bottles on the counter. 'You've no idea how difficult it was to get some of these things before.'

It took quite a time to get Mrs Venables's order together, and to pack it away in Bronwen's silver carrier bags with witches' symbols all over, but it was done at last and Sally hurried back into the workroom. It was almost lunchtime now, and she must get the potion bottled before the rush began.

The mixture was still bubbling merrily in the cauldron, with the blades slowly stirring it round. Sally looked at her watch, but could not remember what time she had turned the cauldron on. She glanced at the recipe again. Boil for 6¼ minutes, it said. It had been boiling for at least that long, she was sure, but she decided to leave it a bit longer while she put the labels on the bottles, just to be on the safe side. The labels were printed by the computer, but luckily Bronwen kept a stock of the common ones.

When the bottles were all labelled and lined up, ready, Sally turned the cauldron off, hinged the stirring blades back out of the way, and carefully poured the steaming liquid into the bottles.

She cleaned the cauldron, put everything away and took the bottles into the shop. She had barely finished putting them on the shelves when the first of the lunchtime customers arrived.

When the lunchtime rush was over, Sally sat on the stool in the workroom feeling very pleased with herself. If she had not made up the potion she would have had to disappoint quite a few customers. She had sold almost half the bottles of fresh Loose-Knicker-Elastic Drops. It was a pity she daren't tell Bronwen how clever she had been.

Her eyes strayed to the rows of intriguing-sounding ingredients on the shelves over the workbench. Surely there could be no harm in just having a quick peek at some of them. She took down a jar marked 'Marshmallow'. The substance inside was white and gooey-looking. Sally picked a tiny piece off and tasted it. It *was* Marshmallow.

She tried a bottle marked. 'Concentrated Midnight Mist'. The cork came out with a plop, and a stream of vapour squirted out and clung to the ceiling. Sally gulped, and put the cork back quickly.

The jar marked 'Shadow of Bat's wing' seemed empty, and so did a vacuum flask labelled 'Frost, Gathered on Hallowe'en'. But a sort of warm, rustling, twittering silence seemed to fill the room when Sally opened 'Warmth of a Summer's Day', and she was almost sure she heard the sound of a cricket ball being struck by a bat.

'South Wind' was empty, too, and so were the jars of West Wind, East Wind and North Wind. Sally wondered if Bronwen knew that she had run out of these things, but of course she dared not tell her, or Bronwen would know she had been peeping at things she had been told not to touch.

She jumped guiltily as the shop door-bell jingle-jangled, but then she realised that it could not be Bronwen. It was far too early. Anyway Bronwen would come through the back door. Sally went into the shop.

'It's him!' snapped a woman, holding tightly on to the hand of a small boy who

was pulling and tugging, trying to get away from her. 'He's getting too big for his boots. Can you fix him?'

'Certainly, madam,' said Sally, taking a jar from the shelf. 'Just rub this on his boots. They'll soon stretch to fit his feet.'

'What good will that do?' exclaimed the woman. 'I want him cut down to size!'

'Oh, I see,' frowned Sally, not really seeing at all. Why on earth would anyone want a child made to fit his shoes, rather than the shoes enlarged to fit the child? Still, Bronwen said that the customer was always right, even when they were wrong. She put the Tight Shoe Spread back on the shelf and, after a little thought, handed the woman another jar. 'Rub him all over with that,' she said.

The woman paid Sally and left, dragging the boy behind her.

'Don't want that smelly stuff all over me!' he screeched, and aimed a kick at another customer who was coming in through the door. The man skipped hurriedly out of the way of the foot that was aimed at his shins, and stumbled backwards into the rack of broomsticks.

'Sorry,' he apologised.

He grinned sheepishly when he saw that it was only a display he had blundered into, but gaped in astonishment when one of the broomsticks said. 'That's all right, sir. It wasn't your fault.'

Then he jumped as a sudden gust of wind blew the workroom door shut with a loud bang. Sally frowned. She was sure the door and window in the workroom were closed. She had better check when she had served this customer.

With wide-eyed backward glances at the broomsticks, the man crossed over to the counter.

7 *An Ill Wind*

'Er, are you the witch?' asked the man, rather hesitantly.

'I'm afraid Bronwen's out, sir,' said Sally. 'Can I help?'

'Oh, well, I, er, don't think so.'

'Well, come back tomorrow, then,' suggested Sally. 'Bronwen will be here then.'

'I–I don't think I could come back,' stammered the man.

'Then tell me what the problem is,' said Sally. 'I'd love to help if I can.'

'Please,' she said, when he hesitated, and looked as if he was about to bolt for the door.

'I–it's–my–nose,' the customer said in a rush, and blushed.

'Your nose?' Sally looked at it, wondering what was wrong with it. It looked perfectly all right to her.

'You see, you're laughing at it,' he said sadly. 'Everyone does.'

'No, really I'm not,' Sally said. 'But what's the matter with it?'

'It's too small. It's a horrible, stupid little bump.'

'It looks perfectly normal to me,' said Sally.

'You're only saying that. You're laughing at me.'

'Honestly I'm not,' said Sally. 'But if you really do want it bigger, it's no problem. I'll give you a potion.'

But then she remembered that she had sold the last of the potion at lunchtime. 'But we'll have some more in the morning,' she said.

'I can't come back tomorrow,' said the customer. He knew she only wanted him to come back so that the witch could have a good laugh at his nose, too. He turned to leave.

'Just a minute!' called Sally. 'There is another way. I could cast a spell.'

There was a loud crash from the work-room. She must see what was going on in there as soon as possible, but she dared not leave this customer, or he would take fright and go.

'And I could walk out of here with a proper nose today?' he asked, his face brightening.

'It will only take a few minutes,' Sally assured him. She took a spell-book from a shelf and led him into the treatment room. He sat down in front of the mirror, while Sally looked up the spell and plugged in the electric wand.

She had never cast a spell before, of course, but she had seen Bronwen do it often enough, and it seemed quite simple. And she had had no problems in mixing up the potion this morning.

Holding the spell-book in one hand and the wand in the other, she chanted;

'Little snout,
Must fill out,
No more woe,
Proboscis grow,
Pto.'

Hoping that she had pronounced the last word properly, Sally tapped the man's nose with the wand, and they both jumped as tiny sparks flew.

'There,' she said. 'That should do it. Now, if you'll excuse me, there's something I must see to.'

She left the man watching his nose in the mirror, and hurried out. The workroom door was rattling and shaking alarmingly. Apprehensively Sally turned the handle and managed to push it open a little. The door was suddenly wrenched from her grasp and crashed back against the wall. Sally screamed.

The workroom was in chaos. Howling, whirling, rushing winds swooshed around in all directions. Swirls of mist formed, to be instantly torn apart. The violently gyrating air was chill and warm in turn. Dark mysterious shadows lurked in the corners of the room. A cacophony of hooting filled the room, almost drowning the gentler sounds of birds twittering and the soft click of a cricket ball on a bat.

Stock from the shelves lay scattered across the floor, and Sally heard crashes behind her as the escaping winds hurled things from all the displays in the shop. The air in both rooms was filled with madly orbiting leaflets and paper, and the artificial cobwebs on the displays were ripped to shreds.

Then the back door flew open and Bronwen forced her way into the workroom against the miniature gale, carrying her briefcase and broomstick.

'Sally!' she cried in horror. 'What have you done?'

'I–I'm sorry, Bronwen!' sobbed Sally. 'I

didn't think there was any harm in just looking!'

Bronwen pushed past her and opened the shop door, to allow the winds to escape. Gradually the noise died down, and the papers settled on the floor, like giant snowflakes. Silently they both set about clearing up the mess. Bronwen just could not bring herself to speak, she was so angry.

The shop doorbell jingle-jangled, and Bronwen, who was sweeping broken glass into a dustpan, stood up. The man who had just come in was very red-faced, and looked as if he was in pain. He held out a bottle of Loose-Knicker-Elastic Drops.

'Your young lady said this was all right for men's underpants,' he said in a strained voice.

'Yes, that's right,' said Bronwen. 'You'll be perfectly safe using that.'

'I already have used it,' he said. 'It's agony!'

'It can't hurt you,' said Bronwen.

'It can! It won't stop working,' he said through clenched teeth. 'I can't even get the blade of a pair of scissors between me and the elastic, to cut them off. There'll be two of me by bedtime.'

'It's impossible,' said Bronwen. 'I've had no other complaints, and this bottle is almost the last of a batch I made up a few days . . .'

Her voice trailed off as she noticed that there were quite a few more bottles on the shelf than she remembered from this morning.

'Sally!' she said slowly.

Sally, who had heard the man complaining, appeared in the workroom doorway, fresh tears running down her face. 'There wasn't enough to last the day, so I . . .'

'Tell me exactly how you made it up,' ordered Bronwen.

Tearfully Sally explained just how she had made up the potion, while the man became redder and redder.

'Well, that sounds all right,' frowned Bronwen, when Sally had finished. 'And when you'd done all that, you boiled it for the right time?'

'Oh yes,' said Sally. 'It had at least 6¼

minutes, because I left it to boil while I served Mrs Venables, and that took an awfully long time.'

'Well, that would have been all right,' said Bronwen. 'The timer would have switched the cauldron off. I don't understand what could have gone wrong.'

'Timer?' said Sally, in a small voice.

'Yes, the timer on the cauldron . . .' Then she looked horrified. 'You did set the timer?'

Sally shook her head. 'I didn't know it had one.'

'No wonder it's too strong!' exclaimed Bronwen, turning to the customer. 'Come into the treatment room and I'll soon put you right.'

Sally gulped. She had just remembered something. 'You–you can't go in there! I–I was in the middle of–of something!'

'Well, there's nowhere else, not with all that mess in the workroom!' snapped Bronwen, pushing open the treatment-room door. She screamed, and the man in the treatment room frantically tried to hide his metre-long nose, which was so heavy he was

resting it on the shelf under the mirror.

Then the doorbell jingle-jangled and a woman burst in, dragging a small boy behind her. 'Look what you've done to him!' she shouted at Sally, pointing at the boy, whose clothes seemed several sizes too large.

'Sally?' said Bronwen, looking at her assistant. '*What* have you done?'

'Nothing!' protested Sally. 'She wanted him shrunk to fit his boots. It looks as if the Double-Chin Reducer has worked.'

'You should sack the stupid girl!' snapped the woman. 'I just wanted him cut down to size, he's getting too big for his boots!'

'Exactly!' exclaimed Sally. 'He seems a perfect fit, now.'

Bronwen found it difficult not to laugh, despite the seriousness of the situation. 'I think the lady just wanted him cured of being too cheeky,' she said. 'A little misunderstanding, madam. We'll soon put him right.'

It was long past closing time before Bronwen had finished restoring the boy to his correct size and curing his cheekiness, remodelling the man's nose and dealing with the stream of distressed purchasers of Loose-Knicker-Elastic Drops.

'I'll get my things,' said Sally, going into the workroom, where there was still the sound of owls hooting eerily, and dark shadows lingered in the corners, despite the fluorescent lights.

'I want to talk to you first,' said Bronwen.

'You're only going to tell me I'm sacked,' snuffled Sally.

'That's right, I was . . .'

'Please don't say any more, Bronwen. I know I've let you down, meddling with things you told me not to, and . . .'

'You won't do it again, though, will you, Sally?' said Bronwen, taking some papers from her briefcase.

Sally shook her head sadly. 'If I can get another job, I'll . . .'

She took the papers which Bronwen was holding out to her, and stared at them. They were brochures about the Witches' Training College.

'I got them from the college on my way back this afternoon,' said Bronwen. 'Would you like to go?'

'Aren't you going to sack me?' asked Sally, bewildered.

Bronwen smiled. 'I was going to, at first,' she admitted. 'But then I'd have to get another assistant, and I'd be worried they'd do what you've done today. I don't think I could stand that.'

Sally threw herself at Bronwen and hugged her. 'Oh thank you, Bronwen, thank you!' she cried.

'You'll go there one day a week,' explained Bronwen. 'And it's quite a long way, so you'd better have a company broomstick to get there. You could use it for making deliveries, too.'

She turned to the broomstick rack. 'Fred,

how would you like to be Sally's broom-stick?'

Fred's sad little face lit up with joy, and he danced out of the rack to cries of disgruntle-ment from the rest of the broomsticks.

'You must promise me never to meddle with things you don't understand, Sally,' said Bronwen. 'And that goes for you, too, Fred.'

'I promise, I promise!' cried Sally excited-ly. 'But I still don't understand what went wrong with the nose spell. Didn't I pro-nounce "pto" correctly?'

'"Pto"?' repeated Bronwen. 'What do you mean?'

Sally got the spell-book and showed it to Bronwen. Bronwen laughed.

'Oh Sally!' she said. 'It's not a word! It means "please turn over"! The spell to stop the nose growing when it's the right size is on the next page!'